AMAZING HISTORY

PIRATES

NEIL MORRIS

W
FRANKLIN WATTS

 An Appleseed Editions book

First published in 2007 by Franklin Watts

Franklin Watts
338 Euston Road, London NW1 3BH

Franklin Watts Australia
Level 17/207 Kent St, Sydney, NSW 2000

© 2007 Appleseed Editions

Appleseed Editions Ltd
Well House, Friars Hill, Guestling, East Sussex TN35 4ET

Created by Q2A Media
Series Editor: Jean Coppendale
Designers: Diksha Khatri, Ashita Murgai
Picture Researchers: Lalit Dalal, Jyoti Sachdev
Illustrators: Hemant Arya, Adil A Siddiqui, Amir Khan, Manish Prasad, Prashant Jogi, Subhash Vohra

ISBN   978 0 7496 7534 9

Dewey classification: 364.16' 4

All words in **bold** can be found in the glossary on page 30.

Website information is correct at time of going to press. However, the publishers cannot
accept liability for any information or links found on third-party websites.

A CIP catalogue for this book is available from the British Library.

Picture Credits:
t=top b=bottom c=centre l=left r=right m=middle
Cover images: Bettmann/ Corbis: background, Sherwin McGehee/ Istockphoto: b,
Back cover: Q2A Media: tl, Linda Bucklin/ Shutterstock: tm, Pepbaix | Dreamstime.com: tr
Q2A Media: 4t, 6t, 6b, 9b, 12bl, 13, 14, 17, 18mr, 19, 20, 26t, 27b, 3LH-Fine Art/ Superstock: 4b, Corbis: 5t,
The British Library Board: 7t, Baldwin H. Ward & Kathryn C. Ward/ Corbis: 8b, The Bridgeman Art Library/ Photolibrary: 12br,
Albert Cheng/ Shutterstock: 15, T.W./ Shutterstock: 16, DGID/ Istockphoto: 18bl, Aris Vidalis/ Istockphoto: 18br,
Library of Congress: 21t, 22b, 26b, 27t, Bettmann/ Corbis: 21b, National Maritime Museum, London: 23t, Scott Rothstein/
Shutterstock: 24t, Jubal Harshaw/ Shutterstock: 24b.

Printed in China

Franklin Watts is a division of Hachette Children's Books

Contents

What is a pirate?   4

Barbary corsairs   6

Privateers   8

Caribbean buccaneers   10

Beware, pirates!   12

Pirate weapons   14

Pirate ships   16

Life on the high seas   18

Blackbeard   20

Women pirates   22

Treasure trove   24

Pirate punishment   26

Pirates today   28

Glossary   30

Index and Webfinder   32

What is a pirate?

The word pirate means 'robber at sea'. For as long as ships have crossed the oceans, taking goods from one port to another, there have been pirates eager to rob them.

Thieves at sea

Stories and films often show pirates as exciting adventurers, but most of them were just blood-thirsty thieves! Many pirates chose their way of life because they thought it was a way to get rich quickly and some men were criminals escaping the law; others were kidnapped and forced into a life of piracy.

Pirate flag
The skull-and-crossbones also called the **Jolly Roger**

Fierce attack
Pirate leaders were brutal, desperate men

Pirates attacked ships for gold, jewels, sugar, spices, tobacco, medicine and rum.

Chinese pirates sailed Asian seas in armed junks. They sometimes attacked European ships in groups.

EUROPE
France
Italy
Spain
• **Algiers**

AFRICA

Bamboo
Strengthened
the junk's sails

Pirate hunting grounds

When Spain controlled the South American colonies in the 1500s, Spanish treasure fleets came under attack. Barbary pirates or **corsairs** had bases in Algiers and attacked ships from Spain, France and Italy. In the early 1600s, Asian pirates attacked European ships. Fleets of Chinese pirates terrorized the coast in the 1800s. The Indian Ocean became the pirates' hunting ground, when ships of the East India Company traded between Europe and Asia in the 17th and 18th centuries.

HOTSPOTS

The famous pirate Captain William Kidd was hired as a privateer, but he turned to piracy and made a fortune robbing ships in the Indian Ocean.

Barbary corsairs

During the 1500s bands of sea robbers called corsairs worked along the **Barbary Coast**, North Africa. They looted ships and sold crews into slavery.

Ruthless red-beards

Aruj and Kheir-ed-Din were the most feared Barbary corsairs. They had red beards and were called the 'Barbarossa' brothers. Both led big corsair fleets. Aruj was killed in 1518 by the Spaniards, but his brother fought on against the Christian enemies.

Kheir-ed-Din, one of the fierce Barbarossa brothers.

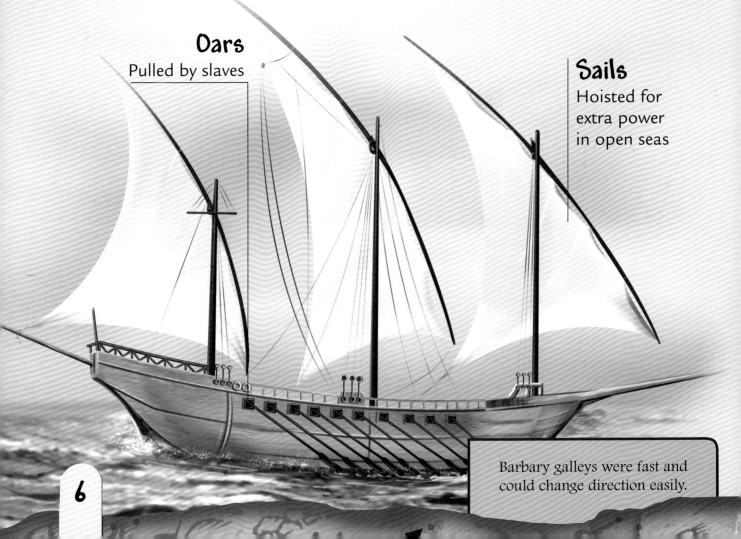

Oars
Pulled by slaves

Sails
Hoisted for extra power in open seas

Barbary galleys were fast and could change direction easily.

Pages from a book called *The History of the Barbary Corsairs*, written in 1637. The pictures show the various methods of torture the Corsairs used on their captives.

Turning Turk

Most of the Barbary Coast was under **Muslim** rule. The corsairs were after treasure from the ships as well as Christians to sell into slavery. In the 1600s, many Europeans joined the Muslims. Dutch pirate Simon Danziger and **privateer** Jan Jansz joined up with the Barbary corsairs. Jansz raided Iceland, and captured and **enslaved** at least 400 islanders. In 1607, English **nobleman** Sir Francis Verney 'turned Turk' and joined the Barbary corsairs. One of his prizes included an English trading ship that was carrying French wine for the king's table.

HOTSPOTS

The name Barbary comes from the Latin and Greek for 'foreign' or 'strange'. It is related to the word 'barbarian', which the Romans used for all foreigners who lived on the outskirts of their empire.

Privateers

Queen Elizabeth I of England hated Catholic Spain and she wanted Spanish treasure. The queen was happy for her sea captains to raid Spanish ships bringing back gold and silver to Spain from captured lands in South America.

Pirating hero

Elizabeth's favourite 'pirate' was Francis Drake. For 30 years he led one attack after another on the Spanish fleet, **plundering** enemy ships and collecting a fortune. In his ship the *Golden Hind*, Drake regularly attacked Spanish treasure **galleons**. He presented Elizabeth with jewels, 13 chests of golden dishes and tonnes of silver and gold.

Elizabeth I thanked and honoured Drake by knighting him on board the *Golden Hind* in 1581.

Licence to steal

Governments gave out **licences**, called '**letters of marque**', which allowed sailors to attack and rob enemy ships. Seamen who had such a letter could not be accused of piracy, which was punishable by death. Instead those working for a government were called privateers. Unlike pirates, privateers had to share their stolen booty with their king or queen.

Mainmast
The largest mast with the biggest sails

The *Golden Hind*, in which Sir Francis Drake sailed around the world. The ship was 36.5 metres long.

Crow's nest
Where a lookout could stand

Caribbean buccaneers

Around the early 1600s, outlaws from Europe escaped to the Caribbean islands. These offered an excellent hideout. The first **buccaneers** were French adventurers who lived on **Hispaniola**.

Meat smokers

The buccaneers took their name from the French word *boucan*, a grill for smoking meat. They lived a fierce life, hunting wild boar and selling dried meat to passing ships for gunpowder and supplies. When they discovered that hunting ships brought bigger prizes, they decided to become pirates. More and more ruffians, convicts and escaped slaves soon joined them.

Treasure galleon
Slow and difficult to sail when fully loaded

Boarding vessel
Out of the galleon's firing line

A pirate boarding party approaching a treasure ship in the Caribbean. Pirate ships were usually smaller and faster, and able to catch their prey quickly once they had spotted it.

Henry Morgan attacked towns in Central and South America. He forced his victims to give up their treasure – or face torture or death.

Henry Morgan

Welshman Henry Morgan (1635-88) gathered a pirate army and led raids on Spanish ships and colonies. Licensed to rob, he destroyed Panama City (the largest Spanish city in Central America) in 1671. He attacked with 38 ships and 2,000 men. This suited the British, and King Charles II made him a knight and deputy governor of Jamaica. Sir Henry collected a fortune as a royal pirate, but drank himself to death.

HOTSPOTS

Frenchman François L'Olonnais (1630–68) was a particularly cruel buccaneer. He was known to hack his victims to death with his cutlass and then lick the blood from the blade.

Beware, pirates!

Pirates watched ports closely to find out which ships had the richest cargoes. They knew the routes treasure ships took and lay in wait for their prey in shallow waters. Pirates preferred to capture their enemies without a fight.

Surprise attack

Pirates often followed their victims for days, keeping just out of sight. Then they would suddenly appear, fire their cannons and shout and generally make a lot of noise. Pirates tried not to damage the ship in case they could use it for themselves, especially if their own ship was damaged.

Grappling hook

French privateer Robert Surcouf used his small, fast ship to attack and capture *The Kent*, a much bigger British ship in the Bay of Bengal in 1800.

Taking the ship

When they were at close range pirates aimed cannonballs at the enemy ship. Then they sailed alongside the ship and threw grappling hooks into the **rigging**. The sharp hooks caught in the ropes. The pirates pulled the ships together and jumped aboard, screaming and shouting. There was fierce fighting but the pirates usually outnumbered the crew and took their prize.

The three stages of a pirate ship's attack were fast and furious.

First the pirates fired at the victim.

Then they pulled in close...

HOTSPOTS

Pirates sometimes tricked their victims by flying a friendly flag as they sailed towards them. Then, when it was too late to escape, the pirates would run up their black flag and, if there was no surrender, they would attack!

... and leaped aboard, armed to the teeth.

Pirate weapons

Pirates used a wide range of weapons to capture the ships they boarded. But first they had to get on board.

Cannonballs

Pirates fired iron cannonballs to stop and damage enemy ships. A cannonball that struck the opponent's **hull** could cause a lot of injuries to the crew from flying splinters of wood. Another tactic was to use chain-shot. This involved chaining two cannonballs together and firing them at enemy masts and sails to bring them down.

One...
Ram gunpowder into the barrel

Two...
Roll in a cannonball

Three... Fire!
Light the fuse

The gunner loaded a cannon and then fired it from a gun port on the main deck.

Flintlock and cutlass

Flintlock pistols were the pirates' favourite boarding weapons. They had a short barrel and were easy to carry. But reloading was slow, so most pirates did not bother and just clubbed the enemy with the hard butt end. In hand-to-hand fights, pirates also used the cut-throat **cutlass** to slash at their opponents and daggers to stab them.

When the trigger of a flintlock pistol was pulled, the flint inside struck a metal plate. This created sparks that lit the gunpowder and fired the shot. The longer musket was fired from the shoulder.

Cutlass
A short, broad blade with a hand guard

Musket
Used before boarding to kill the man steering the enemy ship

Flintlock pistol
Light and easy to carry

HOTSPOTS

At close range, pirates often threw stinkpots on the deck of the enemy ship. These were small, clay pots that were usually filled with a burning mixture of tar and rags. These caused clouds of foul-smelling smoke, which created panic and made the eyes water.

15

Pirate ships

What makes a good pirate ship? The answer is... SPEED!
Most pirates did not build their own ships, but simply stole
those that they captured. They then added extra guns or
changed the rigging to make them faster.

Topsail
Provided added speed
when necessary

Speedy sloops

From the early 1700s pirates went after
speedy **sloops** and larger **schooners** with
big sails. Up to 75 pirates could squeeze
on board and these ships carried 14 guns.
They were perfect for the hit-and-run
techniques of the pirate trade. Single-
masted sloops were favourites with
Caribbean pirates.

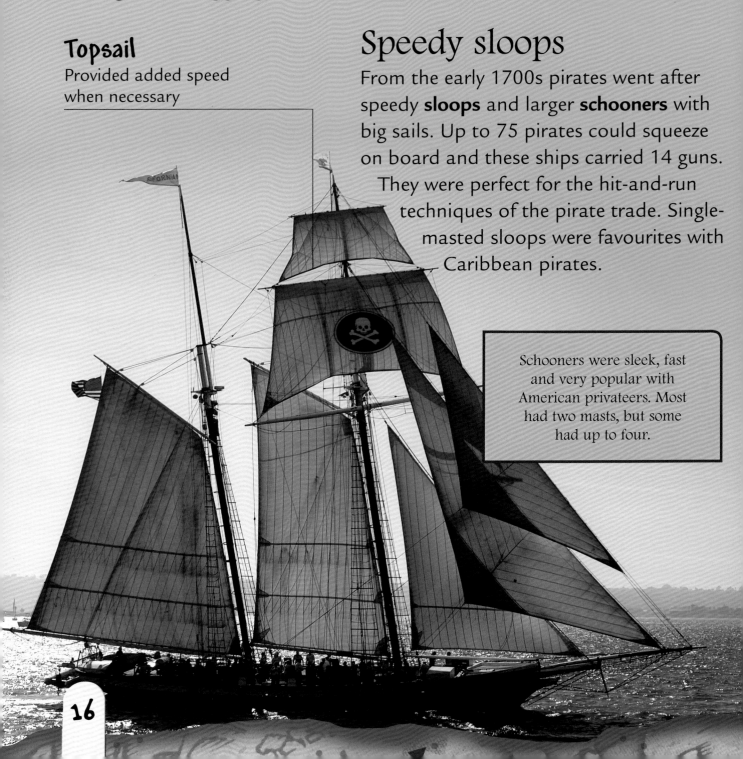

Schooners were sleek, fast
and very popular with
American privateers. Most
had two masts, but some
had up to four.

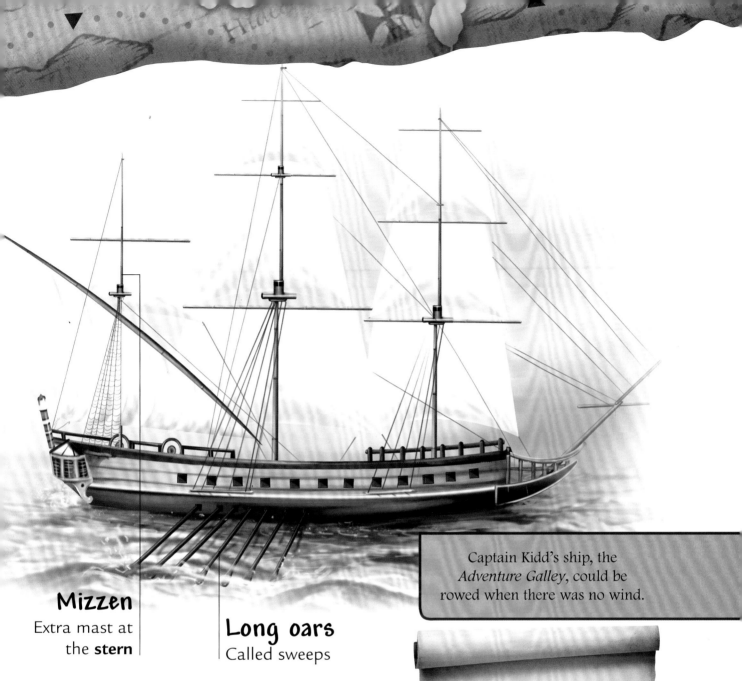

Mizzen
Extra mast at
the **stern**

Long oars
Called sweeps

Captain Kidd's ship, the
Adventure Galley, could be
rowed when there was no wind.

Adventure galley

The *Adventure Galley* was built in 1695
for William Kidd, the famous Scottish-
born privateer, to hunt pirates – before
he became one himself. The ship was
38 metres long and could reach a speed
of 14 knots (27 kph). It had 34 guns
that fired twelve-pounders (weighing
5.4 kg each), and Kidd's crew had
1,000 spare cannonballs for refills.
Unfortunately, this brilliant ship had
problems with leaks!

HOTSPOTS

*Chinese pirates captured
cargo ships and fitted
them out with guns and
cannons. Big fighting junks
were about 30 metres long
and could cram in up
to 400 men. The junk's
sails were made of
bamboo matting.*

Life on the high seas

Life on board a pirate ship was tough and dangerous. At night the crew slept in the small, smelly hold. Water slopped below and there were rats everywhere.

Hard tack

Long-lasting biscuits made from flour and water were pirates' basic food. These biscuits, known as hard tack, were stale and usually full of wriggling weevils. It was best to eat them in the dark and wash them down with gulps of beer. Sometimes there was dried, salted meat, but this was hard to chew. Some crews kept chickens for their eggs, which they called 'cackle fruit'.

Beer
Kept better than fresh water

Turtle meat
A pirate delicacy

Biscuits
Hard and tough

Sour medicine

Fresh fruit and vegetables did not keep on long sea journeys, and many pirates fell ill with **scurvy** due to a lack of vitamin C. In 1753 it was discovered that eating limes could prevent the disease. Conditions on board were filthy, and sickness and infection spread easily. Injured limbs were just sawn off – usually by the ship's carpenter and without any painkillers.

Medical supplies were precious and rare.

Surgery
Patient had to be held down

It was best to avoid injury. Surgery was basic and extremely painful.

Blackbeard

Edward Teach was known as Blackbeard. He terrorized the North American coast and was one of the fiercest men in the history of piracy. In 1717 he **blockaded** Charleston, in South Carolina, plundered ships and kidnapped rich citizens.

Huge terror

Blackbeard was a huge man. He twisted the ends of his beard into plaits and tied them with ribbons looped over his ears. He carried several pistols and sometimes fired them under the table while eating with his crew. Blackbeard once filled the hold of his ship with sulphur fumes to see how long his crew could stay there. He was so cruel that he drove his own men to mutiny.

NORTH AMERICA

South Carolina

Charleston

Burning hair

Blackbeard plaited pieces of cord into his hair which were set alight, to look more frightening in battle

Swords

Two swords and several knives with very sharp blades

When Blackbeard went into battle he terrified the enemy. He was known for being ruthless and cruel.

Pistols

Three pairs of pistols

Blackbeard's last stand

In 1718, Lieutenant Robert Maynard chased the fearsome pirate with two sloops and 60 men. Blackbeard escaped when the sloops ran aground, calling Maynard's men 'cowardly puppies'. With the rising tide Maynard's sloop broke free and caught up with the pirate ship. In a brutal hand-to-hand fight and after receiving five pistol shots and 20 sword wounds, Blackbeard was killed. Maynard cut off the head and threw the body overboard. It is said that it swam twice around the ship before sinking.

HOTSPOTS

Blackbeard's ship, Queen Anne's Revenge, was the largest pirate ship ever. The wreck was found in 1996 by divers off the coast of North Carolina, USA.

Blackbeard put up a tremendous fight with sword and pistol before he was finally killed.

Blackbeard's head was hung on Maynard's ship for all to see.

Women pirates

Women were not welcome on board pirate ships. But they fought just as bravely and were just as ruthless as male pirates. Adventurous women, such as Anne Bonney and Mary Read, dressed up as men and became pirates.

Bonney and Calico Jack

Anne Bonney fell in love with pirate captain Jack Rackham, called Calico Jack because of his coarse cloth trousers. She dressed up as a man and joined Jack's crew. Rackham was hanged in 1720. Anne Bonney was let off because she was pregnant. When Calico Jack was at the gallows, she told him: "Had you fought like a man, you need not have hanged like a dog!"

This was the flag of pirate captain Jack Rackham, which showed crossed cutlasses instead of bones.

Mary Read (right) made friends with Anne Bonney (left) when Calico Jack captured her ship. From 1718, the pair raided Spanish treasure ships.

The Chinese pirate leader Madame Cheng was a fierce warrior. Armed with a cutlass, she feared no man.

Madame Cheng

In the early 19th century the South China Sea was controlled by Ching Shih, who became known as Madame Cheng. She was the widow of Cheng I, who controlled a vast fleet of pirate **junks**. Between 1807 and 1810 more than 70,000 pirates **looted** under Madame Cheng's ruthless command – she punished any theft by beheading. In 1810 she bought a pardon from the Chinese government.

HOTSPOTS

About 1,500 years ago Goth princess Alvilda from Sweden sailed off with an all-woman crew to avoid marrying a Danish prince. They became pirates and preyed on ships along the coast of Denmark.

Treasure trove

Pirates were always on the lookout for valuable goods that were easy to sell. Their favourite treasure was gold, silver and precious jewels. They found all these on ships sailing back to Europe from the Americas.

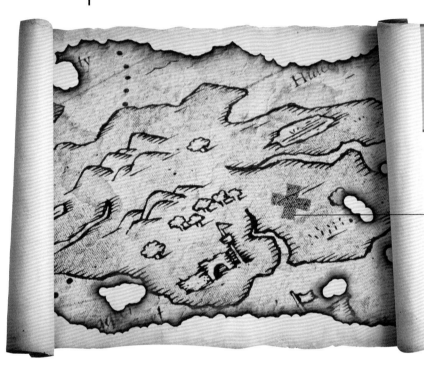

Many pirate maps have been found over the years but few of them are real.

X marks the spot
Where the treasure was buried

Doubloon
The most valuable Spanish gold coin

Cross
Used as a guide to break the coin into halves or quarters

Buried treasure

Pirates generally looked for a quick sale for their **booty**, but sometimes they had to hide it away. There have been many tales of hidden **hoards** but these were mostly myths. However, Captain Kidd really did bury his treasure, but not on a desert island. In 1699 he hid his loot on Gardiners Island, just off New York. Most of it was found, but some has never been discovered.

Coins from Spain and other countries were popular with pirates for their precious metals, as well as for what they could buy.

Captain Kidd made sure he buried his treasure before he was arrested for piracy.

Captain Kidd
Keeps a sharp eye on the burial of his treasure

Crew
Dig a deep hole to bury the booty

Treasure chest
Marked WK for William Kidd

Sharing the spoils

A hold full of gold was every pirate's dream. The captain and his officers usually received a special share of the loot, but otherwise it was split evenly among the crew. The spoils were usually divided as 2 shares for the captain, 1½ shares for the ship's master and doctor, 1¼ shares for the first mate, gunner and **boatswain**, and 1 share for ordinary crew members. The loot might be worth millions of pounds at today's values.

HOTSPOTS

Welsh pirate Henry Morgan raided Panama City in 1671, but his buccaneers found little loot to share. In 1927 hoards of gold and silver were found in the Church of San José in Panama. Perhaps the treasure had been hidden in the church before Morgan's attack.

Pirate punishment

Pirates always hoped that their crimes would pay. But very few lived to enjoy their wealth, and throughout history captured pirates faced a horrible death. In Roman times they were crucified, and in later centuries they were beheaded or hanged.

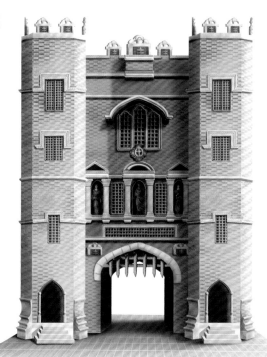

Newgate Prison, in London, was a fearsome place. Kidd was held there for a year.

Captain Kidd's corpse was hung from a wooden frame called a gibbet.

Horrible warning

In England, pirates were tried and then usually executed. In 1701 William Kidd had to go through his hanging twice, after the first rope snapped. His corpse was chained to a post over the River Thames, to be washed over by the tide three times. It was then covered in tar and put in an iron cage to serve as a horrible warning to would-be pirates.

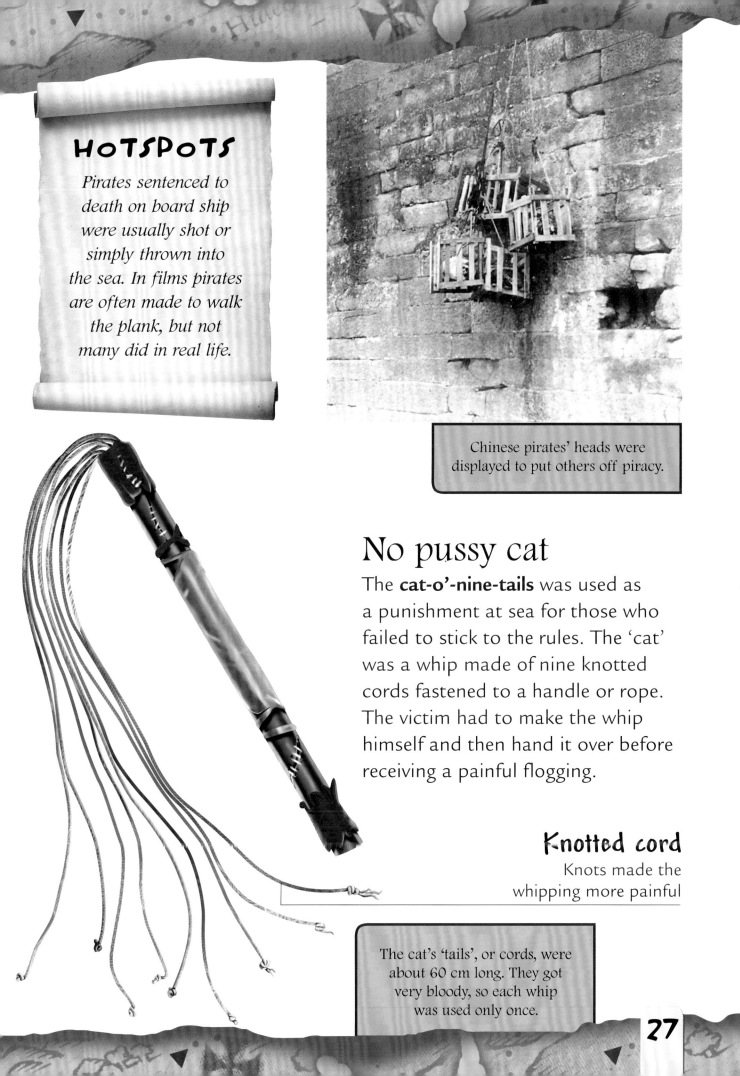

Chinese pirates' heads were displayed to put others off piracy.

No pussy cat

The **cat-o'-nine-tails** was used as a punishment at sea for those who failed to stick to the rules. The 'cat' was a whip made of nine knotted cords fastened to a handle or rope. The victim had to make the whip himself and then hand it over before receiving a painful flogging.

Knotted cord

Knots made the whipping more painful

The cat's 'tails', or cords, were about 60 cm long. They got very bloody, so each whip was used only once.

Glossary

Barbary Coast The Mediterranean coast of North Africa.

blockade To prevent people entering or leaving a place.

boatswain Pronounced bosun, a ship's officer in charge of equipment.

booty Valuable stolen goods.

bow The front part of a ship.

buccaneer A pirate or privateer who raided Spanish ships and colonies in the West Indies.

cat-o'-nine-tails A whip used for flogging.

corsair A pirate or privateer of the Mediterranean region.

cruise liner A large passenger ship that takes holidaymakers on a voyage.

cutlass A short sword with a curved blade.

enslave To make someone a slave.

flintlock pistol An early gun in which a flint spark lit gunpowder.

galleon A large three-masted, sailing ship, used especially by the Spanish.

galley A large ship powered by oars (and sometimes sails).

global positioning system (GPS) A network of transmitters and space-satellite links that can pinpoint a ship's location.

Hispaniola A large Caribbean island (today making up the countries of Haiti and the Dominican Republic).

hoard A hidden store of valuable goods.

hull The main body of a ship.

Jolly Roger A pirate flag.

junk A Chinese sailing ship.

letter of marque An official licence giving authority to attack enemy ships.

licence Official, written permission.

loot To steal goods.

musket An early gun with a long barrel.

Muslim A follower of the religion of Islam.

navigate To follow a course and find the right way.

nobleman A man who belongs to a high social class.

pieces of eight Spanish silver coins.

plunder Stolen goods.

privateer Someone who is legally authorized to attack enemy ships.

ransom Money paid for the release of a prisoner.

rigging Ropes that support a ship's masts and control the sails.

run aground (of a ship) To hit the seabed in shallow water.

satellite navigation (satnav) A method of finding your way by information from space satellites.

schooner A small, fast two- or three-masted sailing ship.

scurvy A disease caused by a lack of vitamin C. Sailors caught it by not eating enough fresh fruit and vegetables. Scurvy caused bleeding gums and sores on the skin.

sea-lane A route at sea that is regularly used by ships.

sloop A small, light single-masted sailing ship.

stern The rear part of a ship.

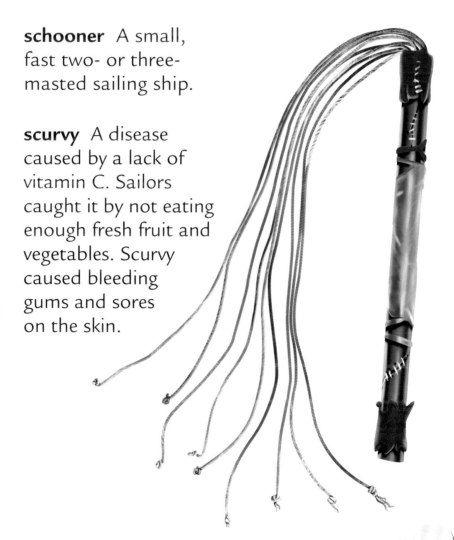

Index

Adventure Galley 17
Anne Bonney 22

Barbarossa brothers 6
Barbary Coast 6–7
Bartholomew Roberts 19
buccaneer 11

Calico Jack 22
cannon 14
Caribbean 10, 16
cat-o'-nine-tails 27
Ching Shih
   (Madame Cheng) 23
corsair 6
cutlass 11, 15, 23

East India Company 5
Edward Teach
   (Blackbeard) 20–21

flintlock pistol 15
Francis Drake 8–9

galleon 10
galley 17
global positioning
   system (GPS) 29
Golden Hind 8–9
grappling hook 12
gunpowder 10, 14–15

hard tack 18
Henry Morgan 11, 25
Hispaniola 10

Jack Rackham 22
Jolly Roger 4
junk 5, 16–17

letters of marque 9

Mary Read 22
musket 15

privateer 5, 7, 12, 17

Queen Anne's Revenge 21
Queen Elizabeth I 8

Robert Maynard 21

schooner 16
scurvy 19
sloop 21
stinkpot 15

treasure 5, 7, 8, 10–11,
   12, 22, 24–25
treasure ship 10

weevil 18
William Kidd 5, 17,
   25, 26

Webfinder

www.thepiratesrealm.com – Lots of information about famous pirates, ships and flags.

www.nationalgeographic.com/pirates – National Geographic presents a High Seas Adventure.

www.nmm.ac.uk/server/show/conWebDoc.159 – Information from the National Maritime Museum, with a link to a Time Pirates adventure game.

www.thewayofthepirates.com – Includes life stories of Blackbeard, Calico Jack and Sir Francis Drake.

disney.go.com/disneypictures/pirates – Website of the Disney film *Pirates of the Caribbean*.